CORBYN

First they ignore you...

Contents

	Introduction	Page 4
1.	June	Page 20
2.	July	Page 36
3.	August	Page 52
4.	September	Page 80
	Conclusion	Page 92

Introduction

As I write this in the lead up to Christmas 2015, British aircraft are bombing Syria. For many reasons, I was opposed to the airstrikes, one reason being I did not consider the argument for airstrikes was justified without further debate, and another being fear of a repeat of the Iraq War. But, regardless of my views, I could not bring myself to openly criticise those who deemed airstrikes necessary; for it was an impossible decision to make either way. A decision of conscience beyond measure.

    The press were locked in a fascinating battle of democracy: one side eager to present the facts, some more than others, and the other side eager to distort particular views on the matter. Far be it for me to politicise such an important issue, it serves to highlight the tug-o-war that is British politics. A stark reflection of our democratic system with the British press at the heart.

In a similar vein, delegates of the Paris Climate Change Conference are currently patting each other on the back for doing only a fraction of what could and should be done for the future of humanity; yet another example of how the media often confuse the difference between reporting the news and reporting their own version of the news. For example, there is a strong possibility that George Osborne is sitting at home in his smoking jacket, sipping fine wine, and wielding his quill in another attempt to deprive Britain's poorest communities of a future; but whether this can be considered news is another matter. Another example would be this: somewhere inside the political machine we call Westminster, there is a man conjuring up ways to defend the rights of the ordinary people of Britain... whilst pinching himself... and scratching his beard... and measuring up for a new Lenin hat — the new leader of the Labour Party, Jeremy Corbyn. Again, not news. But if you read any number of the daily papers, you would think it was.

After spending thirty-two years as a Labour backbencher, which is arguably the perfect training ground for any potential future Prime Minister, Corbyn knows his way around the political scene. Having repeatedly won the support of his Islington North constituency and voicing their concerns in parliament, Corbyn stands by the traditional values they seek in a Labour Party parliamentary candidate. Some would argue he has been too traditional and failed to "move with the times"; but there is something to be said for a man who, having seen the Labour Party's gradual shift from a union backed, community driven, party of the working people, to a corporate funded, individualist, party of the middle classes, Corbyn, in all that time, has remained true to himself and to the party. His vision is not one that denounces financial success or the people that achieve it, but, rather, one that says people who have been fortunate enough to achieve success should pay their fair share into the state that helped them achieve their success in the first place.

Having consistently campaigned alongside the Stop the War Coalition, promoted peace-talks across the world, and been forthcoming in his socialist beliefs that teach us of compassion, community, and comradeship, there can be no doubt where Corbyn's values lie. And as one who has been ignored by the mainstream media and Blairites of New (now old) Labour — an ignorance that led to the travesty of the 2003 Iraq War which Corbyn predicted would lead to further violence and terrorism — Corbyn, at last, has a platform from which he can state his case to the people of Britain, whoever and wherever they are.

In a world of corporate-run governments, the profiteering rhetoric of privatisation creeps ever deeper into our health service, housing and education sectors — three pioneering bedrocks of British life that led the world by example in their foresight, and are envied across the globe. For many years the "profit over people" agenda has been the agenda for those on the Right of the political spectrum, whilst the Left held firm as best they could in keeping the flame burning; for it is easier to dismantle something than build something, and the constant defence of British infrastructure has meant the Left, whilst under constant attack from the Right, have struggled to agree a way forward. This has meant that the right-wing of Parliament have had an all-too easy time under David Cameron. And Corbyn's recent rise to prominence is in reaction to this.

Ed Milliband, who was undoubtedly a better option for Labour than his right-wing brother David, tried his best; but, ultimately, he did not have the resilience to see off Cameron and his best Fleet Street buddies; for if you are going to promote socialism to a Murdoch-controlled, Capitalist, ultra-conservative, right-wing media, you better make sure you come with a strong argument and backbone to match, as well as a better vision for the future than your opponent; all of which Ed did not have. Milliband was torn between his socialist beliefs, held dear by traditional Labour voters, and those of New Labour. And this conflict came across in Labour's rhetoric during the 2015 General Election (GE). The rhetoric was along the lines of "We want the same as the Tories, but slightly different", when it should have been "The Tories are ruining everything we've built, our way is better".

Corbyn, on the other hand, , is a man totally opposed to almost everything the Tories stand for. With his scruffy hair, dodgy beard and cheap suits, he seems able to handle whatever the press throw at him: surely there are only so many times they can print nonsense about Corbyn, right? Maybe, maybe not. But one thing is for sure — he knows what he wants and, after thirty-two years, he has the patience.

As a student of English Literature, and with a view to teach secondary school children, I feel a strong sense of moral responsibility for both the profession I seek to represent and the children I hope to teach during their transition from child to adult. And it is this desire to teach the English language to future generations that inspired me to write this book. Language has an important role to play in binding communities, shaping cultures, and building future prospects of every member of society, regardless of class, race, or gender. It has the power to distract and cohere, propagandise and persuade, and is always the defining characteristic in the way battles are won and lost; for one to win a battle, one needs support, and support is won through language. And language is why, in my opinion, Jeremy Corbyn proved such a popular proposition to the Labour Party membership.

While Yvette Cooper, Liz Kendall, and Andy Burnham were decent candidates, they mistake was to repeat the same dull rhetoric that saw Ed Milliband lose the General Election. Corbyn, on the other hand, talked about issues that people wanted to hear; he spoke to them about a true alternative to austerity and the plundering of the Tory government; he showed the people, and other members of the Labour Party whether they wanted to hear it or not, that democracy only works when you have at least two opposing ideas; for it is all very well saying there is no point in disagreeing for the sake of disagreeing, but, to my mind, that is exactly the same as saying "Well, we might as well just have one party in Britain from now on". Opposition is critical, and this is where the British press come in.

The British press are an important part of society. With news content constantly changing the way it reaches the end user, and with social media giving instant access to global reports, the press are arguably even more important today than they have ever been. The language they use shapes opinion and helps to both inform and, consequently, form society. Hence, it seems logical that all journalists should feel a certain sense of moral responsibility towards the reader, society, and even the language.

There is no doubt that, on political topics, opinion pieces have their place — opinion is paramount in any democracy and I have included some opinion pieces in the narrative — but the front pages of newspapers, especially the headlines, should have a moral awareness of the crucial influence they have on the reader and society as a whole. Therefore, it seems odd to see the front pages of newspapers, whose journalists, by and large, are mostly Oxford and Cambridge graduates, with language unbecoming of an academic and a scholar. Of course, I understand how the world works: when I pick up a paper and turn to the back pages to catch up on what Arsene Wenger has said in his latest press conference, I expect the language to be aimed at the man or woman on the street; when I turn to the centre pages to read the One Direction interview, I expect the language to be watered down; and when I browse the classifieds, I know the language has to be short and snappy to grab my attention and sell me their product; all of that is fine and completely understandable. But when I read about something as important as war, healthcare, education, housing, or the welfare state, to name a few, I want to be told the facts, with a clear measured opinion within the body of the text. I do not want to be scared into thinking one thing by the headline and then told something else in the body of the text. If I want satire, I turn to Frankie Boyle or a number of other comedians; for fully-fledged opinion pieces I turn to Owen Jones and other high-quality writers whose job it is to offer their opinion; but the front pages should be there to inform the public of the latest news, not subject it to propaganda.

Propaganda is to be expected from all political parties. After all, it could be argued that propaganda is merely an extension of persuasion, and it is in party interests to persuade people to vote for them. But when a broad range of newspapers, of which the sector is edging ever closer to a Murdoch monopoly, actually resorting to lies, then that is too far over the line. The press have a responsibility to language, to society, and to democracy.

Jeremy Corbyn has been an MP for Labour since 1983. As one of the most experienced members of parliament, there is no doubt he has served his Islington North constituency well. But until June 2015, the sixty-six year old was repeatedly ignored by the mainstream press for reasons which are possibly less than credible. As a supporter of traditional Labour values, Corbyn has always asserted himself with dignity, repeatedly standing up for what he believes to be right, even if it was considered unpopular within Labour Party ranks. The same, of course, could be said for David Cameron, but it is fair to say that Cameron's treatment in the press is remarkably tame compared to Corbyn's.

When Sinn Fein were supporting the IRA bombings in London, Corbyn took the difficult decision to invite Gerry Adams, leader of Sinn Fein, to London for a meeting to discuss a peace process; in 2003 when Tony Blair, then Prime Minister and leader of the Labour Party, declared war on Iraq, Corbyn was one of the few MPs to oppose the bombings, asking the government to continue its search for a peaceful solution. Yet, his words were masked from public opinion and ignored by the

Parliamentary Labour Party (PLP). Even now, knowing what we know, many parts of the British media refuse to give the Labour Left, which, as well as Corbyn, includes longstanding MPs such as John McDonnell, Dennis Skinner, and Diane Abbott, any credit. Certain newspapers still feel the need to ridicule Corbyn for what they deem to be "pacifism". It is a shame that the Establishment, which, among others, includes Westminster and the British press, seem hell-bent on leading Britain down the path of corporate control and handing over the peoples' best interests to a bunch of far-right oppressors whom choose not to report the arguments on both sides, but, rather, to promote their own agenda.

What I have attempted to do with this book, therefore, is highlight merely a tiny proportion of the struggle Britain and The West faces in the fight against the Capitalist agenda of "profit over people". It is my tiny contribution in highlighting just how impressive Corbyn's rise to prominence was, and just how important it could be for our children, grandchildren, and future generations that Corbyn is remembered throughout history as someone who never ceased fighting for what he believed.

This book, however, is not an attempt on my part to ridicule individual journalists, for all of whom I have great respect in the work they do under strict instructions from their editors. Their dedication and skill is way beyond my own. But for the language to change, the hierarchy within corporate media firms must change; and for that to change, the government agenda must change. Through the medium of the press the narrative comes alive, and their coverage of the Labour Party leadership contest was extensive and remarkable. I hope this book goes some way in showing British media's adroitness.

    This text is not a comprehensive overview of the British media. It merely attempts to analyse the media narrative over a three-month period between June and September 2015 — from the day Jeremy Corbyn announced his intention to enter the Labour leadership contest, to the day after he was elected leader. All of the headlines are presented in their original format and have remained unaltered, so as to give an accurate account of the timeline. In deciding which headlines to include, for, of course, there were many thousands, I have chosen to stick with certain publications I feel capture the mood of the Labour Party leadership contest. I have been very careful to choose stories from a wide range of UK sources. Again, I must reiterate that it is not a complete and comprehensive media account of the leadership race — that would be way beyond the remit of this book and would require multiple volumes — but, rather, more of a factual narrative that presents a broad view of the events which took place.

The conflicting ideologies of the British media is an extremely important part of the text. Conflict is critical in any democracy, but it is important to remember that many factions of British society, be them on the Left or Right of the political spectrum, usually read only one newspaper a day, and some people merely glance at the headlines. This is a shame because politics is all about getting a broad view of ideas and not sticking to just one view. I hope reading this will inspire people to, in future, get a broader view of the political climate before passing judgement or jumping on the back of political whirlwinds whipped up by the British press. This is what I hope. Hype should be created by the people, not by the media. Of course I understand that views will differ, but, again, that is democracy and I can live with that.

At this point, full disclosure — I am a member of The Green Party of England & Wales, and I do not agree with all of Corbyn's views, or, indeed, all of The Green Party's views for that matter. But if this book can assist people in forming a considered opinion, as well as considering the huge task MPs have in getting their message across, I am content in the fact it has achieved what it set out to do.

Lastly, I will say this: Corbyn's rise to prominence during those few short summer months was a triumph for the British public. It was a triumph because it showed that, regardless which paper said what about who, the public made up their own mind about Corbyn. And making up one's own mind, coming to one's own conclusions, shows that maybe the papers have less power than they thought. It is a true sign of democracy in a world full of tyranny.

'First they ignore you, then they laugh at you, then they fight you, then you win'

— misattributed to Mahatma Gandhi

1

June 2015

June 2015 saw the beginnings of Jeremy Corbyn's campaign to become the next leader of the Labour Party. It was also the start of a media campaign which saw Corbynmania, as it came to be known, engage sections of society which previously felt a disconnect from politics. And as someone who grew up with *Oasis* and *Blur* on the front pages, I found it fascinating. Corbyn's rise from backbench obscurity to leader of the Labour Party was immense and, towards the end, was attracting rock-star crowd-levels not seen in my lifetime. Sure, General Elections usually have a good turnout, but for a contest to determine the leader of a political party to gain such momentum is unheard of.

Prior to June, very few people had heard of Jeremy Corbyn. Within the constituency of Islington North there is no doubt that ears would prick at the mention of the Labour MP's name, but to anyone living outside the urbanised area of inner-city London, the phrase 'Jeremy who?' would have been the general response. Serving as a Labour backbencher since 1983, Corbyn was largely ignored by the British press. There are many reasons for this, but I'll leave those discussions to people like Owen Jones and Andrew Neil to argue over.

What is more interesting, though, is the resilience of the British public. With a barrage of information arriving daily to potential voters' mobiles, tablets, and TVs, I feel I can do no more than congratulate the British public who go about their daily life refusing to bow under the pressure of the Murdoch-fuelled sector we call media. Of course, I understand Mr Murdoch has hard-boiled reasons for supporting one particular ideology over another, but I am amazed by the sheer audacity in which his newspapers persistently promote his bias. It goes way beyond freedom of speech or freedom of the press and, in my opinion, borders dangerously on slander, though I admit I am no legal expert. But, rather worryingly, his papers claim to represent the voice of the people. Really? Most people I know agree with virtually none of the claims made on the front pages of *The Sun*.

Margaret Thatcher said, "If they attack one personally, it means they have not a single political argument left". And it would seem, surprisingly, to be exactly the thing her own party, the Conservative Party, and the British press, are doing to Jeremy Corbyn — attacking him personally... and he only came to power recently. Are the British press really so afraid of his policies that they have to start with the personal attacks so soon? It took them at least a year before they started attacking Ed Milliband personally... wait... no, actually...

Corbyn's family, heritage, education, and even his beard — things are rarely about the politics, and when they are they are negative. "Communist!" they shout; "Terrorist sympathiser!" they scream; "He's a socialist!" they cry, as if socialists are in some way linked to the devil. Where is the reporting? Where is the questioning that is essential to any democracy? While Cameron is supported in the British press for his desire to go to war, Corbyn is lambasted for his desire for peace. Hardly a coherent argument on the part of the press. And don't get me wrong, I do not blame any of the MPs whom voted for airstrikes for doing so. It was clearly a vote of conscience either way. But how the press can label the Left as self-righteous, and then then label Corbyn as a pacifist is the essence of irony.

Told in four parts — June, July, August, September —the first part, June 2015, could be considered as the British media attempting to offer a mere taste of Corbyn. At this point, nobody thought he would win, but there is a real sense that, although it is ridiculous to even consider such a "loony-lefty" taking charge of Her Majesty's Opposition, if he does, Labour's chances of a 2020 GE victory would be dashed. So, his chances of winning are played down, almost to the extent where his candidacy is considered a joke.

Some papers bury Corbyn's comments deep in the latter pages, as if ignoring him will help the other candidate. Others choose to attack the man they see as the enemy head-on. But, regardless of their views of him, at this stage Corbyn is by no means public enemy number one. There is, however, a sense of panic within the narrative of some newspapers — a kind of "But what if...?" feel.

THE INDEPENDENT — 4th June
'Anti-austerity' left-winger Corbyn to join Labour leadership race

From day one Corbyn's position is made clear: he's left-wing. While the other candidates are labelled Centrists or Moderates, Corbyn is clearly seen as the ultimate anti-Tory — a position which would have won him many supporters within the Labour Party membership and, indeed, across the UK.

But while people on the Left would have welcomed Corbyn's leadership bid, Moderates within the party and across the country would have seen the "left-winger" language as discouraging and, possibly, even untrustworthy. The narrative of Corbyn being "too" left-wing is already in motion with most of the mainstream media.

THE SUN — 5th June
Corbyn's nuke bid

The Sun certainly have a way with words. The harsh language from this headline does not fully reflect the article content. Evocations of warfare are present here and dangerous connotations relating to fear are alluded to. This is a typical headline for

The Sun because the word "nuke" catches peoples' attention by exploiting their fear.

THE INDEPENDENT — 15th June
Prescott leads calls to keep left-winger Corbyn on ballot

Shortly after announcing his candidacy for the leadership contest, Jeremy Corbyn faced a backlash from the Parliamentary Labour Party. With Corbyn borrowing votes from other Labour MPs who would not have voted for him, many MPs saw Corbyn's ticket as unfair. However, John Prescott and the Labour Party membership argued that it was done in the spirit of democracy and that party members wanted a real debate over which direction the party should go in the 2020 General Election (GE) — Left or Centre.

But once the other candidates, Yvette Cooper, Liz Kendall, and Andy Burnham, realised just how right-wing they looked when standing next to Corbyn, they decided to cause a stir.

Here, Corbyn receives some big-name backing from former Deputy Prime Minister John Prescott — a comment that was welcomed by the Labour Party membership too.

YouGov Polling

Date:	16/06/2015
People polled:	448
Like/Really Like:	42%
Don't Like/Really Don't Like	38%
OK/Unsure	20%

Early polling by YouGov shows Corbyn's popularity across the UK. It is important to remember this is a poll of people across the UK, not just within the Labour cohort.

What is clear from this poll is that Corbyn is liked and loathed in equal measure. In fact, his polling statistics are not altogether different from those of David Cameron. However, the "OK/Unsure" figure of 20% highlights what Corbyn must do if he is to win the Labour leadership — he must aim to convince the Centrists, or the people who have no opinion either way. If he can win them, if elected as Labour leader, he stands a real chance of winning the 2020 GE.

THE SUN — 16th June
Firebrand Corbyn is on ballot for leader

The term firebrand, although meaning someone who is passionate about certain causes, is a harsh word that many people would have to look twice at. Even at this early stage in the campaign, it is clear that *The Sun* will not be backing Corbyn, and, in some ways, he is still considered to be the "joke candidate".

THE GUARDIAN — 17th June
Jeremy Corbyn: 'I don't do personal'

The media's attempts to cause a stir among the Labour Party leadership candidates stumbles at the first hurdle. For while the political arena has in recent years taken a negative approach, Corbyn states his intentions for a clean, democratic debate early on. This is a clever tactic from Corbyn because it shows how serious and focused he is on the campaign, whilst shutting down the media desire for big headlines.

The other candidates follow suit, but they find it difficult to promote their vision, mainly because their vision is difficult to differentiate from the

Conservatives. So, as Corbyn removes the tactic of mudslinging, his rival candidates must choose between being seen as either the negative candidate or the candidate who is not anti-Tory — and no Labour voter wants a Tory-loving leader.

THE SUN — 20th June
UNIONS BACKING CORBYN AS CHIEF

This headline is the first time Corbyn is shown to be the candidate with the support of the people. The Left would definitely read this as a boost for workers rights, but the Right, and possibly even the Moderates, would find this unnerving.

Public opinion regarding unions has shifted since Margaret Thatcher's period in office; for while many people still support the unions and see their position as a key part of a fully democratic society, there are many on the Right, and even Moderates, who see the unions as nothing more than a hindrance to business and Capitalism.

So, while this headline may seem to show Corbyn in a good light, the Moderates are the ones who are targeted here.

THE INDEPENDENT — 22nd June
For just £3, you could help make the Corbyn fantasy come true

When the press discovered anyone could sign up to the Labour Party membership, they pounced on it immediately. Suddenly there was a real sense that Corbyn could quite possibly become leader, but for all the wrong reasons.

Many papers started reporting that anyone, literally anyone, could sign up. The idea was that Tory, Ukip, and Liberal Democrat voters from all over the country should vote for Corbyn, thereby destroying the Labour Party forever. This highlights the contempt the British media had for Corbyn.

In an embarrassing attempt to mock Labour's democratic process by implying that if he won, it would only be because people who thought he was a joke had voted for him so Labour would be destroyed as a political force forever. Of course, the Labour Party membership reached 400,000 by the time of his victory, and after many voters were vetted, all rumours of foul play were quashed.

THE GUARDIAN — 23rd June
In Labour's leadership race, Yvette Cooper is the one to beat

Corbyn received most of the applause at the hustings which were held up and down the country, but the press still insisted on reporting other candidates were favourite to win, even though all the empirical evidence suggested Corbyn was most popular. It was as if they picked their candidate from the start and said "that's who we want, so that's who we'll force the public to vote for". A bizarre strategy, but that is the papers for you.

THE INDEPENDENT — 24th June
Burnham favoured to revive Labour fortunes - but young prefer Kendall

The Independent give a more balanced view in this headline, but still it is hard to see where Corbyn fits in. Apparently "the young", as sweeping a statement as it is, favour Kendall and Burnham is still the favourite.

The truth is, Burnham is favourite with the bookmakers at this point, and Kendall, because she is the youngest and very much an individualist Blairite who seems to be "all about the money", is portrayed as the winner of the young vote. It is important to remember that, at this stage, nobody has voted, and a large majority of young Labour members are in support of Corbyn.

What June's papers show, is the media's refusal to give a fair hearing to all party members in the headlines. Of course, some of these were opinion pieces, but who the paper chooses to print is very important to the media narrative because it shows democracy in full flow.

CHAPTER REFERENCES

Grice, Andrew, and Nigel Morris. "Anti-Austerity' Left-Winger Corbyn To Join Labour Leadership Race'. *The Independent* 2015: 10. Print.

Grice, Andrew. 'Burnham Favoured To Revive Labour Fortunes - But Young Prefer Kendall'. *THE INDEPENDENT* 2015: 8. Print.

Hattenstone, Simon. 'Jeremy Corbyn: 'I Don't Do Personal''. *THE GUARDIAN* 2015: 6. Print.

Hawkes, Steve. 'UNIONS BACKING CORBYN AS CHIEF'. *THE SUN* 2015: 4. Print.

McSmith, Andy. 'Prescott Leads Calls To Keep Left-Winger Corbyn On Ballot'. *THE INDEPENDENT* 2015: 8. Print.

Norman, Matthew. 'For Just Pounds 3, You Could Help Make The Corbyn Fantasy Come True'. *THE INDEPENDENT* 2015: 28. Print.

Schofield, Kevin. 'Firebrand Corbyn Is On Ballot For Leader'. *THE SUN* 2015: 2. Print.

Sun, The. 'Corbyn's Nuke Bid'. *The Sun* 2015: 2. Print.

2

July 2015

After a flurry of reports throughout June predicting Corbyn as nowhere in the race, July was where the narrative begun changing direction. As if from nowhere, Corbyn started to receive backing from major players. Unions from all sectors were coming out in public and showing their support for the man they saw as saving the public sector. And like any good drama, in true Second-Act style, the British press realised Labour Party members might actually be on their way to electing an ardent socialist as leader of Her Majesty's Opposition.

Of course, in true to form, the press upped their rhetoric on the Corbyn campaign from "dismissive-verging-on-ridiculous", to "time-to-get-real". Literally overnight the general tone changed: Corbyn went from the token-gesture candidate whose aim was to inspire debate within the party, to the man causing splits within the Labour Party; from leadership candidates possibly offering Corbyn a job in *their* shadow cabinet, to leadership candidates wanting a job in *Corbyn's* shadow cabinet; from Labour MPs having to borrow Corbyn their votes just to get him on the ticket, to swathes of union members promising to vote for Corbyn in their tens-of-thousands. Corbyn went from the MP who Labour's elite ignored for thirty-two years, to being laughed at for a few weeks by the media, to being a danger to society — according to the press, the Tories, and many past and present Labour MPs. They could sense rebellion — or, as I like to call it, democracy — in the British political airstream, and they did not like it one little bit.

In an attempt to make a mockery of the Labour Party leadership contest, certain newspapers continued to call upon non-Labour voters to sign up as Labour Party members for £3 and vote for Corbyn (a scheme that one might consider to be reverse psychology, if it wasn't so damn stupid). Additionally, some newspapers started to panic and pulled out the big-guns with terms like "Red", "Marxist", and "Looney-Lefty", as if this in some way attached Corbyn to Stalin, Lenin, and other names often associated to be being enemies of Western civilisation.

Thankfully, however, many reports were cool and calm, which helped to settle the boat. Big-name political commentators, such as the aforementioned political commentator Owen Jones and comedy genius Frankie Boyle, upped their game in defiance of the gutter press to help steady the ship. But, though they assisted in keeping the narrative focused on the Labour intraparty debate, Corbyn's emergence was quickly becoming a battle of wills between the major left and right wing commentators. With a balanced view across a broad range of newspaper narratives, people would be able to see sense, but without the mix of rationality on the part of writers like Jones, and the exposition of the absurd on the part of comedians like Boyle, people would have been easily sucked into a hate campaign.

Some papers seemed hell-bent on reporting fear instead of facts. It was as if they could see the future and it was full of bearded, hat-wearing, men with copies of the *Morning Star* under their arm; when, of course, what we all prefer are *cleanly shaven*, *top*-hat-wearing, men with copies of the

Daily Mail under their arm *instead*, right? Had the press forgotten their role in British politics? Would they have been happier with two right-wing parties controlling government? Probably. But a democracy only works if you have a dialogue: two opposing ideologies which frame a debate. And, in this case, Corbyn was creating that dialogue by standing against the Blairites within the Labour Party. He was offering a real alternative to voters desperately calling for true opposition to government.

Maybe the media were too used to life under Tony Blair, who many argue was merely a Tory masquerading as Labour supporter, and had forgotten how the whole thing worked. Well, before long they would find out just how little power they had.

THE SUN — 6th July
UNITE BOSSES BACK RED JED: LABOUR LEADER RACE Union's huge boost for leftie Corbyn

Another boost for Corbyn's campaign as yet another union backs him for the top job. But *The Sun*'s focus on unions being associated with "leftie Corbyn" shows their clear intent on evoking feelings of strikes and riots experienced by older members of the voting public. And with unions portrayed as the enemy by the *The Sun,* there is a real chance that Moderate members of the Labour Party will not vote for Corbyn.

The Left, on the other hand, are starting to build momentum.

THE SUN — 11th July
LEFTY CORBWIN FEAR

Come mid-July, there was a real sense that Labour MPs were generally worried about Corbyn getting into power. It was as if the Blairites, who kicked out many of the left-wing dissidents in the party years ago, were suddenly worried about getting a taste of their own medicine. The play on words had to go up a notch in the eyes of many papers, and here is a great example with "Corbwin" — smashing.

THE SUN — 12th July
VERY RED MUCH WED UNION LED: COULD THIS DANGEROUS MARXIST THROWBACK ACTUALLY BE ELECTED NEXT LABOUR LEADER?

While the Labour membership welcomed a change from the Blair-Brown years, many Labour MPs and sections of the press feared a "Marxist" rebellion. With the hustings showing an increasing amount of support for the Corbyn campaign, the mood on Fleet Street was sombre.

Language such as "throwback" and "dangerous" were becoming frequent in many of the right-wing daily rags, implying that Corbyn would take society into a "Stalinist" state of oppression.

THE INDEPENDENT — 13th July
Labour leadership hopefuls attack Harman for backing Tory welfare cuts

At last the other candidates were denouncing Harriet Harman, who was serving in her role as temporary Labour leader following Ed Milliband's resignation, for backing Tory cuts to welfare. The majority of Labour MPs slowly realised what the Labour membership wanted to hear — Opposition.

Corbyn set out his stall from the beginning by stating that he was anti-Tory and anti-austerity, and it took a while for the other candidates to realise this was the way the Labour Party should be. Right-wingers, such as Kendall, and Moderates, such as Cooper and Burnham, were starting to get on board. But it was too late. Corbyn's momentum was surging.

THE INDEPENDENT — 15th July
Labour's tragedy is that Jeremy Corbyn is much the best candidate

This headline captures the general feeling among the British media at the time. Rather than conceding that Corbyn was the standout candidate and inspiring a major Labour movement, instead, the consensus was to ridicule the Labour Party for Corbyn being the best of a bad bunch. At some point the Labour Party would have to concede that the politics of New Labour, which brought success under Tony Blair, would have to change direction.

Labour voters wanted something different. People wanted a new old Labour.

THE INDEPENDENT — 18th July
'You always knew if there was a rebellion, Jeremy would be part of it'

It is true that during his thirty-two years as an MP, out of many thousands of parliamentary votes, Jeremy Corbyn went against the whip on some five hundred occasions. This level of disobedience was frowned upon within a wholly undemocratic "whip" process instilled under Blair and Brown. But now he was having his day in the sun, relishing all that came his way, it seemed obvious that, with hindsight, Corbyn was always going to be the one to lead a so-called rebellion. In fact, all Corbyn was doing was speaking his mind and letting the people choose.

Could it really be seen as a rebellion? After all, Corbyn was a candidate in a democratic election held within democratic political party. It was not as if he had banded together a group of dissidents to form a military coup... he was playing by the book. And that is what seemed to annoy the press and the PLP. For once, someone was playing by the

rules and getting their message out to the people...
and the people liked it.

THE SUN — 19th July
Leftie Corbyn is like Farage...people vote for him as a protest

In many ways, this headline holds water. For it
could be argued that, whoever one votes for, it
automatically is a protest against the other
candidates. Clearly the headline is trying to imply
that Corbyn is a fad, or even a joke, portraying him
as someone people vote for just so the "real" leaders
stand up and take notice. Well, they were taking
notice, alright, of that we can be certain.

THE INDEPENDENT — 20th July
Burnham: I'd serve in Corbyn's Shadow Cabinet if he becomes leader

Interestingly, this is where the mood begins to
change. Some talk prior to this headline was about
whether the other candidates would have Corbyn in
their shadow cabinet or not, but Burnham was the
first one to openly admit he would take a position
in Corbyn's shadow cabinet, should he be elected

(he later took the title of Shadow Home Secretary in Corbyn's shadow cabinet).

Kendell ridiculed Burnham for this, something which made her seem childish and unwilling to listen to others views, which is really not the way to present yourself to a democratic party.

The Left and Right divide of Fleet Street started to become visible, with some papers beginning to discuss Corbyn as a viable option.

THE INDEPENDENT — 22nd July
A joke candidate's a joke candidate, until it gets serious

He was ignored for thirty-two years and laughed at for merely a few weeks before certain journalists realised the joke was on them. Corbyn had arrived on the scene and, to many political commentators utter amazement, people actually liked him. Gosh, whatever could they do?

YouGov Polling

Date:	24/07/2015
People polled:	1150
Like/Really Like	44%
Don't Like/Really Don't Like	42%
OK/Unsure	14%

The polling figures still had Corbyn in the low-mid 40s, but the interesting part here is that the "OK/Unsure" figure is 14% — 6% lower than at the beginning of the campaign. Corbyn was staring to have an effect on people.

THE GUARDIAN — 24th July
Jeremy Corbyn victory would be disaster for Labour, says Liz Kendall

With the general feeling being Corbyn was on the march and attracting backing from all parts of the Labour cohort, Kendall and Co. went from just saying nothing about their stance on certain issues, to still saying nothing about of their political beliefs but with a little negativity about Corbyn thrown in.

It did seem like a strange strategy, especially when hustings' are supposed to be about what the candidate will do for the party, rather than what the other candidate will not.

THE GUARDIAN — 26th July
Why smart Tories should not be smug about Labour's Corbyn-mania

The message was finally hitting home: Corbyn is a man who can win... and not just the Labour Party leadership, but the 2020 GE too. Corbyn-mania was coined and the surge in popularity for the Islington North MP went through the roof.

THE INDEPENDENT — 31st July
Do the Blairites think that Labour should be closed to non-members?

More and more mainstream newspapers started to get on board with the Corbyn campaign, and some even started questioning Blairites within the Labour Party. Suddenly, the Blairites were stuck in the past, reminiscing about a bygone era which included mottos like "We're all middle-class now".

Of course, apart from that statement being literally impossible, neither was it true.

The PLP wanted to have the last say in the selection of Labour leader, but party rules state that members (those people that pay £3 to register) have an equal say to the PLP. The question was rightly being asked of Labour MPs and they failed to answer adequately. Did a democratic party really want to be undemocratic in its voting policy?

This was a battle with only one winner — the people.

CHAPTER REFERENCES

d'Ancona, Matthew. 'Why Smart Tories Should Not Be Smug About Labour's Corbyn-Mania'. *THE GUARDIAN* 2015: 28. Print.

Griffiths, Ben, and Polly Graham. 'VERY RED MUCH WED UNION LED: COULD THIS DANGEROUS ACTUALLY BE ELECTED MARXIST THROWBACK NEXT LABOUR LEADER?'. *THE SUN* 2015: 16. Print.

Lusher, Adam. "You Always Knew If There Was A Rebellion, Jeremy Would Be Part Of It". *THE INDEPENDENT* 2015: 18. Print.

McCann, Kate. 'UNITE BOSSES BACK RED JED: LABOUR LEADER RACE Union's Huge Boost For Leftie Corbyn'. *THE SUN* 2015: 2. Print.

Morris, Nigel. 'Labour Leadership Hopefuls Attack Harman For Backing Tory Welfare Cuts'. *THE INDEPENDENT* 2015: 4. Print.

Norman, Matthew. 'A Joke Candidate's A Joke Candidate, Until It Gets Serious'. *THE INDEPENDENT* 2015: 28. Print.

Norman, Matthew. 'Labour's Tragedy Is That Jeremy Corbyn Is Much The Best Candidate'. *THE INDEPENDENT* 2015: 28. Print.

Robinson, Nick. 'Leftie Corbyn Is Like Farage...People Vote For Him As A Protest'. *THE SUN* 2015: 13. Print.

Schofield, Kevin. 'LEFTY CORBWIN FEAR'. *THE SUN* 2015: 2. Print.

Sparrow, Andrew. 'Jeremy Corbyn Victory Would Be Disaster For Labour, Says Liz Kendall'. *THE GUARDIAN* 2015: 1. Print.

Steel, Mark. 'Do The Blairites Think That Labour Should Be Closed To Non-Members?'. *THE INDEPENDENT* 2015: 34. Print.

Wright, Oliver. 'Burnham: I'd Serve In Corbyn's Shadow Cabinet If He Becomes Leader'. *THE INDEPENDENT* 2015: 6. Print.

3

August 2015

As the Labour Party leadership contest moved into August, a Jeremy Corbyn victory was being bandied about Fleet Street. Support for the Islington North MP began drifting in from all areas of the country and his supporters had something to cheer about, which is more than can be said for his haters.

The former Labour backbencher becomes the focus of "exclusives" and "special reports" throughout August, with newspapers from all sides jumping on the Corbyn bandwagon. Terms such as "Corbynite" and "Corbynomics" enter the mainstream and many papers start to take his vision seriously, with *The Guardian* and *The Observer* leading the charge by looking closely at Corbyn's policies. The beginnings of real, meaningful discussions begin to take place.

On the other hand, papers such as *The Sun*, fearful of real debate becoming a problem, continue with their personalised and, to some extent, unreasonable view of a real alternative to the Tories. Fearmongering becomes rife throughout August and is fast becoming commonplace. It is as if they have no real argument for what Corbyn is proposing, so decide to sling mud instead.

Former Labour MPs, many of whom were influential in the rise of Tony Blair, start writing long, sweeping articles explaining why Labour members should vote for anyone but Corbyn. Of course, knowing what we know about Corbyn's huge victory, their attempts failed, and it becomes clear that the power of the press is losing its battle with the people. Certain Labour MPs, whose ideas under Blair were considered mainstream, were now beginning to get a taste of their own medicine: where once they were the majority, with so-called dissidents such as Jeremy Corbyn and John McDonnell banished from the limelight, the all-powerful Labour bigwigs, such as Blair's former Communications Director Alastair Campbell, were now reeling and did not seem to understand why people were choosing to not listen to what he had to say on the matter. The ideas of Corbyn and his followers were hurtling towards mainstream politics, and there seemed to be nothing the right-wing press could do about it.

What makes the August narrative so interesting is that almost all the papers seem to latch onto just how unprepared both the Left and Right really are: at this stage of the game, the left-wing are still counting on Labour Party factions to do their talking; and the right-wingers are still underestimating Corbyn's appeal; it is as if both sides were unable to deal with the new brand of politics, which was now the new reality; for nobody had any expectations of a Corbyn victory, but, the further into August we go, the more it seemed inevitable that a Corbyn victory was on the cards.

In many respects, the Left are still fuming about all the years of protesting that fell on deaf ears, and Corbyn's campaign team do not seem able to organise activists who now have a real voice — they were not used to being attacked, they were used to being ignored. Similarly, the Right seem unsure what to do, so decide to cover their ears with their hands, close their eyes like a five-year-old, and scream "la-la-la-la I'm not listening to you".

As the drama unfolds and heads towards the final act, the tension builds. Accusations implying Corbyn is a threat to national security come to the fore, and, in an attempt to make him look like an enemy of the state, he is misquoted on several occasions. Tensions within the Labour Party are seized by the media and polemical pieces are once again called upon by the right-wing press in a last gasp attempt to thwart Corbyn's push for victory. But it is to no avail. The people have already decided, and nothing, not even the force of the Establishment, can change their minds.

THE GUARDIAN — 1st August
Jeremy Corbyn supporters risk return to Labour splits of 1980s, says Burnham

Talks of splits within the party become rife throughout August, and Burnham's comparison to the 80s were just the beginnings. Talks of socialist splinter groups breaking off or even forming to make the party larger and more appealing to voters enter the media dialogue, a sure sign that Corbyn was heading for a victory.

THE INDEPENDENT — 3rd August
Corbyn will harm poor, says shadow Chancellor

Burnham joins Kendall and Cooper in their attacks on their Labour colleague. Corbyn, on the other hand, focuses solely on his message to the Labour Party membership and, by doing so, starts to broaden his appeal to the country as a whole.

THE GUARDIAN — 4th August
#JezWeCan: why Jeremy Corbyn gets the social media vote

Twitter started going crazy for all things Corbyn. Avatar accounts of Jeremy Corbyn began popping up all over Twitter and his support seemed never-ending.

However, social media can often give a false picture of events; for many people of the same political values follow each other, so instead of inspiring more dialogue, they end up praising each other and the whole thing just goes round and round in one big ball of praise.

But it cannot be denied that Corbyn's following increased massively from somewhere in the low thousands to 371,000 (as of 17th December 2015).

THE GUARDIAN — 5th August
Win or lose, Jeremy Corbyn has already changed the rules of the game

The idea that politics is not all about winning but, instead, about making a difference and inspiring change is one that many MPs hold true even today.

Caroline Lucas is one example, and Corbyn is another. Themes of "changing the rules of the game" and "the changing face of politics" started to gain pace and became another important factor in Corbyn's rise to prominence.

The argument many Blairites put forward is often about winning elections. They would argue that, in order to make a difference, you have to be in power. But this idea is about-face: there is no easy route to change, it is hard work and then some. You need to build your influence over a number of years and then hope that people engage and follow you. If you win an election on a promise you cannot fulfil, you will end up doing nothing or doing the opposite to what the people have asked of you. It does not work. Furthermore, it can often lead to both the Labour and Tory Party offering similar manifestos, but with little tweaks. For example, in the 2015 General Election, both Labour and the Conservatives were promoting austerity as the way forward; and both were promoting a tougher stance on welfare. Neither party was offering the public an alternative, which is a sign democratic politics in the UK was heading in much the same direction as the United States of America: two parties battling for power instead of two ideologies involved in dialogue for the sake of democracy.

The other downside to having too many similarities between a nation's two main political parties is that both sides, due to having nothing of any substance to argue about, end up resorting to negative politics, by which I mean they start slagging each other off rather than being positive and promoting their own case to the voters.

Jeremy Corbyn was certainly changing politics by saying what he thought to be right, leaving the other three candidates looking dangerously similar to the Tories.

BELFAST TELEGRAPH — 6th August
Labour front-runner vows to bring abortion and same-sex marriage to NI as victims blast refusal to condemn IRA terror

Corbyn has always stood for a united Ireland. And while it may come as a shock to many Brits, one must recognise that Ireland were united before the British invaded, forced residents to speak English, and generally oppressed Irish citizens.

But it seems to me that, although Corbyn's understanding of this difficult area of politics is probably sound, Ireland would not see it that way. Unfortunately, as with all areas of politics, but more so with Ireland, Corbyn's opinion on the matter will be met with contempt.

With the Scottish Referendum done and dusted (for now), it seems inevitable that a discussion over a United Ireland will come up again sometime soon. And with all MPs at some point having to pick which side they are on, frankly, I do not envy them.

But this headline is interesting because it highlights the scale of Corbyn's task if were to win the Labour leadership contest.

THE INDEPENDENT — 7th August
Corbyn: many rich people want to pay more tax

Though to many it might seem that tax is one of those awful things that nobody wants to pay, without it most of us would not be here.

Tax is important for a number of reasons, such as the NHS, education, and transport infrastructure, to name a few, and many rich people realise the importance of it.

And though out of context the headline may seem to ridicule Corbyn, there will be a large number of Centrists and many on the Right who agree.

THE SUN — 8th August
POWER CRAZED: CORBYN'S ENERGY THREAT
Nationalise leccy, gas Plan would cost Pounds 124bn Plan

While the headline reports the figure of £124 billion, it must be said that if the energy companies had not have been sold off in the first place, the government would actually be making money from energy. Consequently, the tax burden for many UK households would be eased. Alternatively, energy prices would be more affordable... a win/win for everyone whichever way one looks at it.

The slow and dangerous emergence of privatisation obsessively sought by the Tories is the real danger to Britons, but because the Tories main interests are to serve the rich, their main concern is wealth creation — something the working classes are often fooled into thinking applies to them also.

Another example of a typical headline by *The Sun*: brash, bold, and exaggerated to extremes.

THE OBSERVER — 9th August
If Jeremy Corbyn becomes leader, will he make the hard calls?

As it starts to become clear that Corbyn is on course for a victory, questions are asked of his resilience. Corbyn is an MP used to leading activists on a march, not MPs into the Commons, so this is a fair question. It is a sign that certain parts of the press are taking Jeremy Corbyn seriously.

THE GUARDIAN — 10th August
Jeremy Corbyn is right to blame the banks, not Labour, for the financial crisis

Many believe one of the main reasons for Ed Milliband's defeat in the 2015 GE was his inability to shift the blame for the financial crash away from the Labour Party and onto the under-regulated banks. The Tories did a good job of pinning the blame on Labour, and Milliband's campaign went along with it to the extent that, at one point, Milliband actually apologised to the nation for Labour "getting it wrong".

Here, *The Guardian* makes it clear Labour were not to blame for the global financial meltdown in its headline and back Corbyn's outspoken views on the issue.

THE GUARDIAN — 12th August
Jeremy Corbyn profile: 'He talks like a human being, about things that are real'

Another hot topic in the 2015 GE was the "likeability factor" of Cameron and Milliband. Whilst Cameron was revered as Presidential, Milliband was lambasted for being out-of-touch and labelled as a bit of a wet fish.

Corbyn, however, though not the sharpest of dressers, by this stage is beginning to come across as a man of the people. He is talking about things that really matter to people and engaging with large parts of the Labour cohort and the broader UK public.

THE INDEPENDENT — 13th August
You Corbynites out there should be careful what you wish for

Corbyn is a new entity, not seen before in British politics. His manner is refreshing and his beliefs longstanding. But it is this fear of the unknown to which many commentators appeal when seeking to sway voters away the other way.

Conversations are beginning to take place over the direction the Labour Party will take under Corbyn. There is talk of Labour "having no chance under Corbyn", and this doubt is reinforced in the rhetoric of this headline.

YouGov Polling

Date:	18/08/2015
People polled:	525
Like/Really Like:	47%
Don't Like/Really Don't Like:	41%
OK/Unsure	12%

With polls consistently showing Corbyn's popularity increasing, left-wing commentators are clearly winning their daily battles with the Right. Furthermore, the "OK/Unsure" category is decreasing further still, meaning, generally speaking, people are being persuaded in favour of Corbyn.

THE GUARDIAN — 18th August
Jeremy Corbyn says antisemitism claims 'ludicrous and wrong'

Accusations start to appear from all angles, but Corbyn shows resilience by refusing to fall into the honey-trap of losing his patience. The words "ludicrous and wrong" show Corbyn at his best: plain talking, no messing about, this *is* and this *isn't*.

The claims do not stick because they are not true. But the aim of the claims are to sling mud and slur Corbyn's name.

THE INDEPENDENT — 20th August
The Labour favourite who knows the words to 'The Red Flag'

More associations with The Red Flag, a traditional Labour song, with evocations of Russia and Stalin coming through. The song has nothing to do with anything other than the Labour Party and its traditional socialist beliefs, but every now and then the press like to remind the public that Corbyn is red, like the devil, or Russia, or... Arsenal?

THE GUARDIAN — 21st August
Jeremy Corbyn to apologise for Iraq war on behalf of Labour if he becomes leader

Whilst Milliband may have been wrong to apologise for the financial crash of 2007/8, Corbyn was certainly not wrong to apologise for the Iraq War on behalf of the party. Everyone knows the war on Iraq was a mistake, but Corbyn and the Stop the War Coalition campaign group knew it then and urged Blair not to go ahead. Blair failed to listen.

Hence, an offer of an apology if he is elected leader is a good way for Corbyn to set the record straight and, more importantly, disassociate himself with the Blair-Brown years. Corbyn realises that, if he is to stand a chance of winning the 2020 GE, he needs to take Labour in his own direction, building them in his image, per se, and move on from New Labour.

THE INDEPENDENT — 25th August
Green Party offers an electoral pact to a Corbyn-led Labour

The notion of electoral pacts is nothing new, it has been around since time immemorial. Every time a new leader takes the hot seat of a major political party, there is an attempt by smaller parties, for want of a better phrase, to "cut a deal" and share the platform.

On this occasion, however, it could be seen as advantageous for both the Labour Party and the Green Party. The Greens foresee a Corbyn victory in the leadership contest and know that a Labour Party victory in the 2020 GE will very much depend on Labour winning back some support from the many voters who deserted them to join other, more left-leaning parties such as the Greens.

Unlike Labour under Blair, where the party moved from Left to Centre and were able to hijack many Tory votes, under Corbyn, Labour would not have much chance of doing the same. Therefore, by making an electoral pact, or going one step further and joining forces with parties such as the Greens, the Liberal Democrats, and possibly even the SNP, in a Labour-led, anti-Tory, Left-coalition would make sense.

However, the chances of this coming to pass is highly unlikely and wholly impractical due to the fundamental difference in priorities between the aforementioned parties. It takes a great deal more to unite a coalition than simply being "anti-Tory".

The headline, on the other hand, offers a stark reminder to the British public about Corbyn's way of thinking. In other words, the rhetoric suggests that Corbyn has more in common with Caroline Lucas and Natalie Bennett than he does with many Blairites. This, to people such as myself, is no bad thing, but to many Moderate Labour voters, it just might be enough to scare them over to a Tory or Ukip vote in the 2016 by-elections and beyond.

BELFAST TELEGRAPH — 26th August
Corbynomics not as unpopular as Right likes to think

With the Right blindly defending Capitalism, it leaves much of the British public oblivious to any possible alternatives. And while ten million Britons did not vote in the 2015 GE, it only goes to show how disassociated ordinary people are with politics and all that goes with it. The idea that most people are for Capitalism is nonsense — most people do not even understand how things could possibly be any different because, in their lifetime, things have never been any different. Explaining the pros and cons of Capitalism to a voter who has no interest in politics but votes because he heard something on the radio about it, is like explaining the pros and cons of Albert Einstein's Theory of Relativity to a Year Seven science class — it means nothing to them because another option does not enter their daily lives. They are used to thousands of people being made redundant while the banks get bailed out; they are used to the poorest sections of society having to choose between buying food or putting on their heating; they are used to paying extortionate prices for their energy whilst receiving some of the most appalling customer service. It is what they are used to because it is all they have ever known. And do not even try to explain an alternative such as Socialism.

But with Corbynomics fast becoming a buzzword, the press latch onto the economist, Richard Murphy, and his blueprint for Corbyn's economic strategy. And though many admit that, while they are not economists, the current system clearly has it faults, so why not look at an alternative? If the human race are to continue moving forward and close the gap between rich and poor, the current "boom and bust" system that is Capitalism cannot continue. Maybe Corbynomics is the way forward.

THE GUARDIAN — 27th August
Jeremy Corbyn: Labour membership will determine policy, not me

The Guardian latch onto Corbyn's main, and possibly most important, strategy. Under Tony Blair, Labour Party policy was decided by the cabinet, or, essentially, the elite members of the PLP. Party members were invited to give their view, but the final say would come down to Blair and Co.

Here, Corbyn's belief that democracy is paramount seems to resonate with the Labour membership. It engages them by reaching out and giving them a voice and a reason to be interested in the party. Corbyn is bringing real change to politics.

THE SUN — 30th August
Corbynomics DON'T work

On the other side of the fence, there are those who say that Corbynomics do not work. Of course, these are mainly Capitalists who are privileged or lucky enough to have been successful under the current system and were probably unaffected by the financial crash. And why should they have been? The people who were affected most heavily were the poor, the workers, and their families.

But here, simply by brandishing a striking headline "Corbynomics Don't Work", *The Sun* kill two political birds with one stone: by attacking the word "Corbynomics", the reader is alienated from both Corbyn and his economic system. An economics is largely where a General Election is won and lost because it affects so many areas of policy.

However, the fatal flaw in this headline, not that it ever stopped the red-tops from printing it, is that nobody knows if Corbynomics would work or not because it has never been tried. And, again, the current system has many catastrophic flaws, so why not try something new? None of us are getting any younger, so let's give it a go.

THE SUN — 31st August
JEZ CALLED BIN'S DEATH 'TRAGEDY'

This headline, on the very last day of August, has to be the most shocking of them all for a number of reasons.

Firstly, out of context it looks bad, but seen in context it actually is not as bad as one might imagine. Secondly, Corbyn is not actually saying anything different to what the Conservative MP Boris Johnson said a few years prior. Thirdly, Corbyn made these remarks in 2011, which makes it quite bizarre that they are only surfacing now... hmmmm...

Corbyn's argument was that, as a democratic nation opposed to violence and in favour of trial by jury, Osama Bin Laden should have been tried in a court of law for his crimes against humanity. And Boris Johnson, only a few months after the horrific 9/11 attacks on the World Trade Center, said of Bin Laden: *"He should be put on trial, because a trial would be the profoundest and most eloquent statement of the difference between our values and his"* (Ridley, 2015).

Johnson's comments are remarkably similar to Corbyn's, who stated: *"There was no attempt whatsoever that I can see to arrest him, to put him on trial, to go through that process. This was an assassination attempt, and is yet another tragedy, upon a tragedy, upon a tragedy. The World Trade Center was a tragedy, the attack on Afghanistan was a tragedy, the war in Iraq was a tragedy... This will just make the world more dangerous and worse and worse and worse. The solution has got to be law, not war"* (ibid).

Considering Corbyn's words were remarkably similar to Johnson's, you would think that *The Sun* would cast all bias aside and report the news as it happens. Unfortunately, this style of propaganda had only just begun.

CHAPTER REFERENCES

Addley, Esther. 'Jeremy Corbyn Profile: 'He Talks Like A Human Being, About Things That Are Real''. *THE GUARDIAN* 2015: 14. Print.

ANON, ANON. 'Corbyn Will Harm Poor, Says Shadow Chancellor'. *THE INDEPENDENT* 2015: 1. Print.

ANON, ANON. 'Labour Front-Runner Vows To Bring Abortion And Same-Sex Marriage To NI As Victims Blast Refusal To Condemn IRA Terror'. *BELFAST TELEGRAPH* 2015: 1. Print.

Boffey, Daniel. 'If Jeremy Corbyn Becomes Leader, Will He Make The Hard Calls?'. *THE OBSERVER* 2015: 1. Print.

Campbell, Alastair. 'You Corbynites Out There Should Be Careful What You Wish For'. *THE INDEPENDENT* 2015: 26. Print.

Cole, Harry. "JEZ CALLED BIN's DEATH 'TRAGEDY'". THE SUN 2015: 4. Print.

Elliott, Larry. "Jeremy Corbyn Is Right To Blame The Banks, Not Labour, For The Financial Crisis". THE GUARDIAN 2015: 21. Print.

Heritage, Stuart. '#Jezwecan: Why Jeremy Corbyn Gets The Social Media Vote'. *THE GUARDIAN*2015: 6. Print.

King, Ian. 'Corbynomics DON't Work'. *THE SUN* 2015: 12. Print.

MacAskill, Ewen. 'Jeremy Corbyn To Apologise For Iraq War On Behalf Of Labour If He Becomes Leader'. *THE GUARDIAN* 2015: 1. Print.

Mason, Rowena, and Frances Perraudin. 'Jeremy Corbyn: Labour Membership Will Determine Policy, Not Me'. *THE GUARDIAN* 2015: 1. Print.

Mason, Rowena. 'Jeremy Corbyn Says Antisemitism Claims 'Ludicrous And Wrong''. *THE GUARDIAN*2015: 4. Print.

McCann, Eamonn. 'Corbynomics Not As Unpopular As Right Likes To Think'. *BELFAST TELEGRAPH* 2015: 23. Print.

Milne, Seamus. 'Win Or Lose, Jeremy Corbyn Has Already Changed The Rules Of The Game'. *THE GUARDIAN* 2015: 31. Print.

Morris, Nigel. 'Corbyn: Many Rich People Want To Pay More Tax'. *THE INDEPENDENT* 2015: 14. Print.

SUN, THE. 'POWER CRAZED: CORBYN's ENERGY THREAT Nationalise Leccy, Gas Plan Would Cost Pounds 124Bn Plan'. *THE SUN* 2015: 4. Print.

Watt, Nicholas. 'Jeremy Corbyn Supporters Risk Return To Labour Splits Of 1980S, Says Burnham'.*THE GUARDIAN* 2015: 1. Print.

Wright, Oliver. 'Green Party Offers An Electoral Pact To A Corbyn-Led Labour'. *THE INDEPENDENT*2015: 10. Print.

Wright, Oliver. 'The Labour Favourite Who Knows The Words To 'The Red Flag''. *THE INDEPENDENT* 2015: 10. Print.

4

September 2015

By September, Corbynmania had reached heights which made Beatlemania seem like Beatle-indifference. On the other side of the fence, the political machine went into overdrive. Fleet Street editors told their teams to get nasty and portray Corbyn as public enemy number one.

But with Corbyn's rise to prominence well on its way, much of the mainstream press had run out of ideas on how to combat Corbyn's vision of a better future. So, they simply rewrote and recycled old articles, which had no effect the first time

around, in the hope that the constant barrage of
abuse would have an effect. Corbyn didn't even
have a chance to buy a new suit or prepare his
victory speech with his comrades before the two
ultra-conservative streets — Downing and Fleet —
decided things had gone far enough. The joke about
Corbyn being like Wolfie from *Citizen Smith* bringing
"power to the people" just wasn't funny anymore. It
was time to get serious. But the team on the Right
could not figure out where they had gone wrong:
hadn't they used all the political tools at their
disposal? Hadn't they offered enough distractions to
keep people on the path of Capitalism? How many
times did they have to explain the "trickle-down
effect" to the working-classes before they got it? It
was as if their daily dose of rhetoric, fuelled by
hacks' egos and Murdoch-owned propaganda guns,
was weakening. Suddenly, Tory-supporting political
commentators reached acceptance of the situation,
and they began planning for the future.

They ignored him for 32 years, then they laughed at
him for a few weeks, then they fought him for a few
more, but now he was going to win... and there was
nothing they could do about it. The people had
made up their own minds — they wanted Corbyn.

The preparation for war had begun. And while many on the Right were regrouping and realigning their strategy, the Left seemed dazed by the awe of it all. The Labour Party was going to be different from now on. It was going to stand for something different than the trickle-down economics that contributed to the boom and bust effects of Capitalism. Corbyn's campaign would refuse to lie back and accept the Conservative way of doing things. They were going to fight for a system of fairness. They were going to inspire a generation. If only they would be given the opportunity to make their case.

TELEGRAPH — 1st September
Jeremy Corbyn campaigned for release of Embassy bombers

With Corbyn facing claims of anti-semitism and associations with so-called extremists, he was fast becoming the target of a major slur campaign from certain factions of the press. Many thought that, at some point, Corbyn would snap and react in the way the press was hoping — with a major outburst.

But he didn't. He simply continued doing what he was doing, much to the frustration of the British press. And his commitment to standing for what he believed was paying off with the voters, regardless of how the press were portraying him.

THE OBSERVER — 5th September
Labour leadership election: MPs prepare to resist Corbynistas

From Corbynites to Corbynistas, Corbynmania was reaching new heights. But, according to many corners of the media, a huge number of Labour MPs were planning to oust him if he won. How strange... the very people that were accusing

Corbyn of being a party rebel were now planning a rebellion.

In reality, it was only a few Labour MPs pushing this idea, but the media were having none of it. As far as they were concerned, Labour was in bits. Media hype at its worst.

THE SUN — 7th September
'Opt out of Army funding'

Corbyn never made a secret of his opposition to war. But the idea that our armed forces would suddenly disappear under Corbyn is a stretch too far, even if that was the implication here.

Corbyn made it clear that defence is important, but many wars could be avoided if diplomatic and political resources are put front-and-centre as the main priority. Taxpayers' option to choose where their taxes were spent seemed a fair idea, and the notion that it should go towards peace instead of war was the declaration made by the leadership contender in 1999. Yet another old story that the press tried to label as "news".

THE INDEPENDENT — 9th September
Corbyn may be just the man to curb this creeping privatisation

Probably the biggest attraction to Corbyn is his staunch opposition to creeping privatisation.

Government funding for the NHS, schools, local councils, social care, and housing is being withdrawn to such an extent that the wellbeing of millions of Britons are at risk. The increasing outsourcing of services to private firms garners a "profit over people" situation where the bottom line becomes more important than the end user.

So, as the Tories continue what Thatcher started and Blair copied, the idea that Corbyn, a man ignored by the media through the 80s, 90s, and 00s, could reverse this injustice is a big pull for many voters.

It helped his campaign for the Labour leadership, but how would it fare with the country as a whole come the 2020 GE?

DAILY EXPRESS — 10th September
8 Shadow Ministers 'to desert Corbyn'

In the lead up to election-day, the then shadow cabinet leaked their disliking of Corbyn to the press. To many, it was no surprise; for when a new regime takes over there are bound to be winners and losers.

But certain parts of the press tried to imply that it was Corbyn who was being "deserted" by his shadow cabinet, rather than he removing them.

A clever ploy, and one that could be recycled over and over again in years to come.

YouGov Polling

Date:	13/09/2015
People polled:	636
Like/Really Like:	47%
Don't Like/Really Don't Like:	42%
OK/Unsure:	11%

With Corbyn's profile reaching every corner of Britain, there was no way his rise in popularity would keep soaring at the astonishing rates that were seen at the beginning of his campaign. But with much of the media portraying Corbyn as a negative influence, it is interesting to think that nobody had changed their mind about him.

The numbers were still good and Corbyn was by no means the disaster that many Blairites were predicting.

THE EXPRESS ON SUNDAY — 13th September
Is this Britain's most dangerous politician?

He did it. The Labour Party had a new leader in the shape of Jeremy Corbyn, and the Left had a new comrade at the top of the British political system.

Despite all the mudslinging, Jeremy Corbyn won the hearts and minds of the Labour Party membership and stormed to a landslide victory, claiming just over 59% of the votes. With the largest majority ever achieved in a Labour Party leadership contest, Corbyn will go down in history, possibly for causing one of the biggest electoral shocks ever known, but definitely as one of the most inspirational figures.

To many, it came as no surprise; for he was by far and away the best candidate with the clearest vision of what the Labour Party should stand for. To others it will be a disaster. But there is no denying that Corbyn has a huge mandate from the Labour Party membership and deserves his place in the hot seat.

The headline, however, signifies the tone of the press going forward. Certainly, many parts of the British press are supportive of Corbyn and would love to see him do well in the 2020 GE; but for the many right-wing factions, and even many Moderates, Corbyn is someone who must be destroyed.

CHAPTER REFERENCES

ANON, ANON. 'Is This Britain's Most Dangerous Politician?'. *THE EXPRESS ON SUNDAY* 2015: 26. Print.

ANON, ANON. 'Jeremy Corbyn Campaigned For Release Of Embassy Bombers'.*TELEGRAPH.CO.UK* 2015. Web. 13 Dec. 2015.

Boffey, Daniel. 'Labour Leadership Election: Mps Prepare To Resist Corbynistas'. *THE OBSERVER*2015: 8. Print.

Brown, Martyn. '8 Shadow Ministers 'To Desert Corbyn''. *DAILY EXPRESS* 2015: 2. Print.

Leftly, Mark. 'Corbyn May Be Just The Man To Curb This Creeping Privatisation'. *THE INDEPENDENT* 2015: 58. Print.

Sabey, Ryan. "Opt Out Of Army Funding". *THE SUN* 2015: 2. Print.

Conclusion

The political arena can learn a lot from the 2015 Labour Party leadership contest, but the main one is this: do not be too quick to write someone off. History has taught us that, from time to time, the most unexpected political candidate has just as much chance of being elected as the so-called favourite. On this occasion, in my opinion, justice has been done. Jeremy Corbyn seems to be the perfect opposition to the hard-line Tory policies driving Britain ever-closer to privatisation. And though nobody wants to see extremes of any political ideology be in power, Corbyn is a welcomed, and absolutely necessary, force for the modern political climate.

Tony Blair was the last, and arguably most successful, Labour leader. But it is worth considering that, for all the good he did for schools and hospitals, he failed miserably on housing and foreign policy: Blair did not build enough council houses to supply increasing demand, and the Iraq War was a disaster that must never be forgotten. But whether Corbyn has enough about him to get into the Prime Minister's hot-seat remains to be seen. Maybe the British press will tread more carefully from now on... I doubt it, but you never know.

As the far-right billionaire Donald Trump goes on the march in America, with his polling improving week-on-week, it is worth remembering that the line between democracy and tyranny is fine. Adolf Hitler, for example, was a madman, but he was a madman with the ability to reach into the heart of society and speak to those most vulnerable to fear-mongering; and way before him was a guy called Jesus, who managed to convince people he was the son of God. My point is that the world has never been without its propaganda merchants selling their own solution to the injustices faced by the masses. But while Corbyn can be compared to none of the above, he has without question proven himself to be a man of compassion with the dedication to fight for the rights of others less fortunate.

Contemporary right-wing politics is struggling to convince people that Capitalism is the best way forward. People are growing tired of a "boom & bust" system fuelled by the apparent human need for wanting more. Many people are finally saying "we don't want more, we want better... we want fairer". And through some weird style of expression that most of us call honesty, Corbyn has managed to fend off the mudslinging and take his place opposite Cameron in the House of Commons. A feat that is remarkable considering the length of time he spent on the backbenches.

The Four-Act drama that was the Labour Party leadership contest is only the first part in a series of democratic dramas for the newly crowned Labour leader. And though Mahatma Gandhi was misattributed with the quotation, "First they ignore you, then they laugh at you, then they fight you, then you win", I felt this was a perfect way to sum up Corbyn's journey. Ironically, the misquote is rather fitting too.

But the cycle has not ended, not by a long shot; for it stands to reason that Corbyn's battles with the press will repeat many times over in the lead up to the 2020 General Election. Already, with it being only three months since he took the reins, Corbyn is struggling to get his message across to the British public. Why? Well, again, others might be in a better position to analyse and answer that question; but I would hazard a guess that the corporate giants' grasp on government policy and media output is so finely intertwined, for the moment, the system is designed to keep the powerful in power.

Over the next five years, Jeremy Corbyn has it all to do. Firstly, he must unite the Labour Party. No mean feat when you consider the Blair-Brown politics many of are used to. Secondly, he has to win over the hearts and minds of the Moderate vote, the Centrists, those voters who are, by and large, indifferent to politics and tend to catch mere snapshots of the latest political goings-on. Thirdly, Corbyn has to make some tough decisions regarding policy; for there is absolutely no chance of Corbyn being able to change the world in one term. He must get the ball rolling, bring people onside, and set things up nicely for the next "Jeremy Corbyn". And fourthly, but by no means last, Corbyn has to find a way of uniting the Left. That means reaching out to other political parties and possibly forming alliances. For too long the Left have been split into tiny factions whilst the Right consolidate and get stronger.

At this point, I must concede that I am not an anti-capitalist; per se; for there are many things, such as the freedom to choose, that Capitalism has taken great strides in promoting. But the laissez-faire brand of Capitalism, which ironically does not believe in state intervention unless it is to bail out financial institutions, is not a system that can continue. It does not do any good for any part of society, except for the financial institutions and the richest 10%. Something has to give.

Ultimately, as previously mentioned, there are three rights every individual should be entitled to from birth: free healthcare, affordable housing, and free education. These rights dwindled under the recent Conservative/Liberal Democrat coalition government, and are in serious danger of disappearing altogether if Cameron and Osborne have their way. Corbynomics, inspired by the economist Richard Murphy, inspires individual aspiration as well as builds a stable economy. And it does all this in a fair and considered approach that has a slightly higher tax levy on the richest ten percent of the country, instead of at the expense of the poor. If an individual is financially successful, they should by all means have their big houses and fast cars and luxury yachts; people have no problem with that. But it makes no sense for the wealthiest people in the country to live like kings whilst the poorest sections of the country starve; for those millions of people at the bottom of the financial ladder are essential to the economy too.

So, what now for the new leader of the Labour Party? Will it be a huge disaster that will see the Labour Party lose its position as Her Majesty's official opposition in government? Or will Corbyn help the Labour Party be the next Syriza or Podemos? The truth is, it is hard to say. Corbyn does not seem fazed by all the press have thrown at him; some would argue he has actually enjoyed the battle. But, truthfully, it is too soon to say. One thing is for certain, though: by fuelling the debate, Corbyn has changed politics for the better.

'First they ignore you, then they laugh at you, then they fight you, then you win'

— misattributed to Mahatma Gandhi

Printed in Great Britain
by Amazon